Overview *A Day at the Trout*

A child goes fishing and learns about trout farming.

Reading Vocabulary Words

fingerlings
alevins
incubators

High-Frequency Words

could	*lakes*
baby	*pond*
next	*bait*
bigger	*catch*

Building Future Vocabulary

** These vocabulary words do not appear in this text. They are provided to develop related oral vocabulary that first appears in future texts.*

Words:	*prepare*	*sections*	*cycle*
Levels:	Gold	Purple	Library

Comprehension Strategy
Asking questions to understand the author

Fluency Skill
Reading smoothly

Phonics Skill
Reading more complex and irregularly spelled words (alevins, yolk)

Reading-Writing Connection
Making a list

MW01715395

Send home one of the Flying Colors Take-Home books for children to share with their families.

Differentiated Instruction

Before reading the text, query children to discover their level of understanding of the comprehension strategy – Asking questions to understand the author. As you work together, provide additional support to children who show a beginning mastery of the strategy.

Focus on ELL

- Have children make their own bulletin board Trout Chart like the one on pages 22 and 23.
- Have children draw pictures on paper plates of the six phases in a trout's life, label each phase, and cut out arrows to show the sequence.

Using This Teaching Version

1. Before Reading

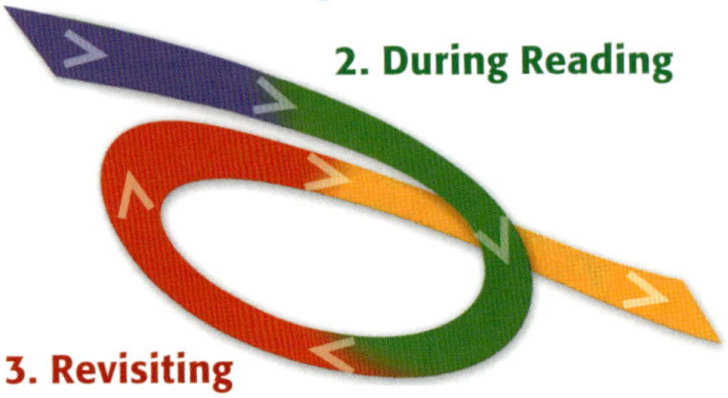

This Teaching Version will assist you in directing children through the process of reading.

1. **Begin with Before Reading** to familiarize children with the book's content. Select the skills and strategies that meet the needs of your children.
2. **Next, go to During Reading** to help children become familiar with the text, and then to read individually on their own.
3. **Then, go back to Revisiting the Text** and select those specific activities that meet children's needs.
4. **Finally, finish with Assessment** to confirm children are ready to move forward to the next text.

1 Before Reading

Building Background

- Write the word *incubators* on the board. Read it aloud. Have children share what they know about incubators. They may not know that eggs are hatched in an incubator.
- Introduce the book by reading the title, talking about the cover photograph, and sharing the overview.

Building Future Vocabulary

Use Interactive Modeling Card: Clues to Use

- Introduce children to Clues to Use, focusing on picture clues. Write the word *sections* in the *New Word* column. Have children page through the book and find images of things with sections.
- Repeat the routine for other words in the text.

Introduction to Reading Vocabulary

- On blank cards write: *fingerlings*, *alevins*, and *incubators*. Read them aloud. Tell children these words will appear in the text of *A Day at the Trout Farm.*
- Use each word in a sentence for understanding.

Introduction to Comprehension Strategy

Activity Sheet: Nonfiction Questions and Answers

- Explain to children that readers who ask questions about what they read understand their reading better and enjoy it more. Ask *What do you know about fish and where they come from? What do you know about fishing? What would you like to find out about these topics by reading this book?*
- As you talk, have children fill in the first two columns of the Activity Sheet.
- Tell children that they will be asking more questions and filling in the rest of the Activity Sheet during the lesson.

Introduction to Phonics

- Write **yolk** on a blank card. Read the word aloud, emphasizing /y/. Ask children to identify the sound they hear at the start of the word.
- Explain that the letter *l* is often silent before letters *d, f, k,* and *m* at the end of words.
- Have children practice saying **yolk** with you.

Modeling Fluency

- Read page 8 smoothly. Tell children that when they read smoothly, the words flow like they do when they talk. Explain that sentence structure and punctuation help them read in phrases rather than individual words.
- Explain that familiarity with vocabulary words such as *alevins* and *yolk* helps them read without slowing down or stumbling as they go.

2 During Reading

Book Talk

Beginning on page T4, use the During Reading notes on the left-hand side to engage children in a book talk. On page 24, follow with Individual Reading.

Book Talk

- **Comprehension Strategy** Ask children if they ever think of a question while they are reading. Say *Good readers are always asking questions before and during reading.*
- After looking at the cover and reading the table of contents, say *I know fish live in water. I wonder if a fish farm is out in the ocean. What do you think?*
- Say *We will probably find the answer to this question as we read the book.*

Turn to page 2 – Book Talk

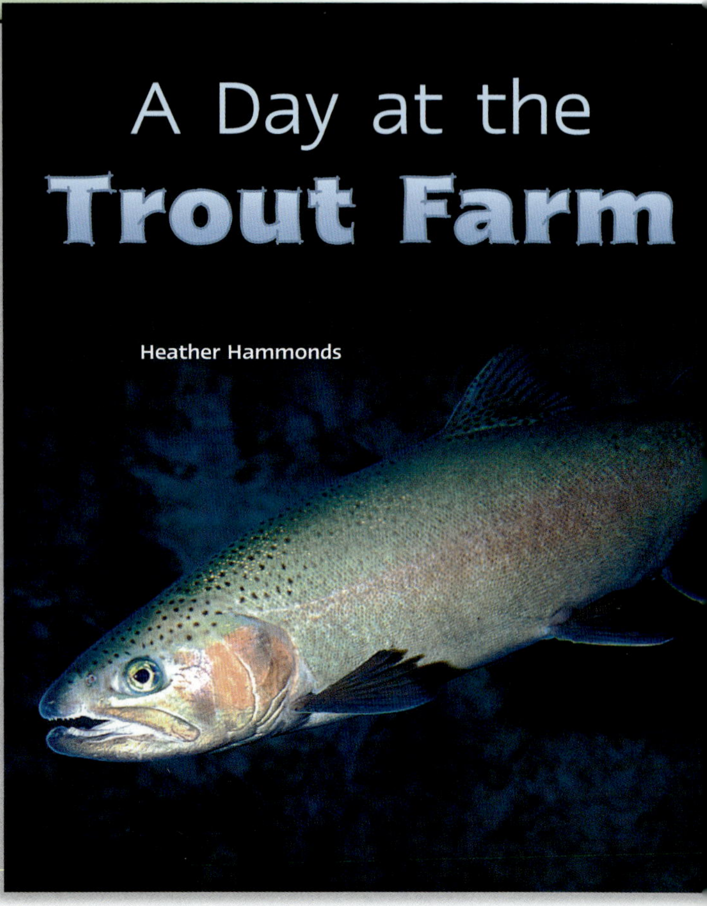

A Day at the Trout Farm

Heather Hammonds

Contents

Chapter 1	Fish for Dinner	2
Chapter 2	A Farm for Fish	4
Chapter 3	About Trout	6
Chapter 4	In the Hatchery	8
Chapter 5	Small Fry	10
Chapter 6	Growing Bigger	12
Chapter 7	Ready to Eat	16
Chapter 8	Fishing for Trout	18
Chapter 9	Our Trout Chart	22
Glossary and Index		24

Future Vocabulary

- Explain to children that the table of contents shows the sections of the book. Say *Chapters are big sections of a book. What other sections did you see in this book?* (glossary, index)
- Say *Looking at the table of contents is a good way to prepare to read a book. How else can we prepare to read?*

Now revisit pages 2–3

During Reading

Book Talk

- **Comprehension Strategy**
  Ask *Is the person who is telling us about trout a girl or a boy?* (girl) *Why do you think that?* (The author is named Heather, and there is a girl in the photograph on the back of the book.)
- Point out the Fishy Fact feature. Say *These Fishy Facts may answer some of our questions. Why do you think these fish are called rainbow trout?* (The photograph on page 3 shows a pink stripe on their bodies.)
- Ask *Does anyone have a question? What are you wondering about?* (Does the girl have a mother? Are the fish on page 3 alive?)

Turn to page 4 – Book Talk

Chapter 1

Fish for Dinner

I like to eat fish.
Dad likes to eat fish, too.

We have fish for dinner every week.

2

Trout is our favorite fish.
We went fishing at a trout farm.
Dad helped me catch some trout!

I learned a lot about trout farming
at the trout farm.

Fishy Fact

There are different
kinds of trout.
This trout is called
a **rainbow trout**.

3

Future Vocabulary

- Tell children that the photograph on page 2 shows one way to prepare trout for dinner. Ask children how they like their fish prepared.
- Explain that a Fishy Fact is a special section of the book that tells important information about trout. Ask *What is the important fact in this Fishy Fact section?*

Now revisit pages 4–5

During Reading

Book Talk

- **Comprehension Strategy** Stop after reading page 4 and ask *What is a pond?* (a little lake; a place for animals to drink) After reading page 5, talk about how text, photographs, and photo labels help answer the question. Say *Sometimes when we read on, we find answers for our questions.*
- Ask *Does anyone else have a question? What are you wondering about?* (What does the word *hatchery* mean on the sign? Does water pollution hurt trout?)

Turn to page 6 – Book Talk

Chapter 2

A Farm for Fish

Dad took me to a big trout farm.
The farm was in the mountains.

There were lots of ponds at the farm.
The ponds were full of rainbow trout.

4

The trout farm was near a river.
The cold, clean water in the trout ponds came from the river.

Fishy Fact

Trout need very clean water to live and grow.

5

Future Vocabulary

- Say *Many kinds of things can have sections. Do you see anything on these pages that has sections?* (the trout pond) *Is the photograph of the trout pond in the top section of the page or the bottom section?* (top)

Now revisit pages 6–7

During Reading

Book Talk

- Explain that words in bold-faced type are in the glossary. Look up *North America* in the glossary on page 24.
- **Comprehension Strategy** Ask *Which photograph on page 6 shows a river?* (lower left) *A trout farm?* (left)
- Point to the photograph of the trout farm. Say *These must also be trout ponds. They look different from the ponds on page 5. I wonder if there are different kinds of trout ponds.*
- Ask *Does anyone else have a question? What are you wondering about?* (Why is the water in each of the trout ponds a different color? How did the people take the eggs to other countries?)

Turn to page 8 – Book Talk

Chapter 3

About Trout

At the trout farm I learned:

- Trout live on trout farms and in lakes and rivers.

- Some kinds of trout live in the sea, too.

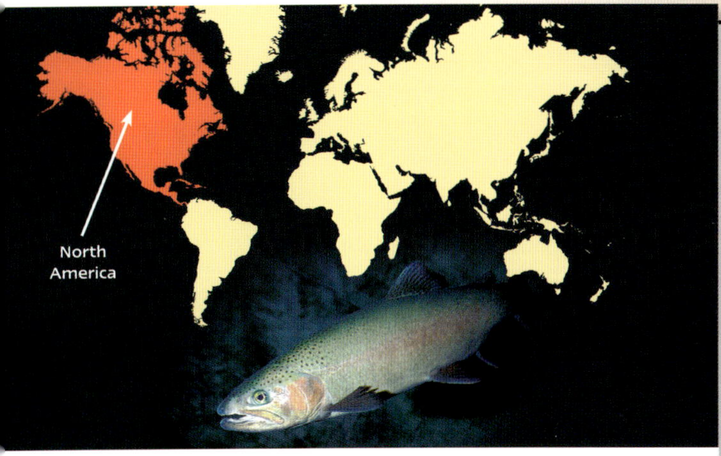

Rainbow trout first lived in parts of **North America**. Then people took the trout eggs to other countries.

Now rainbow trout are found all around the world.

Fishy Fact

Trout like to eat small insects and other fish or water animals.

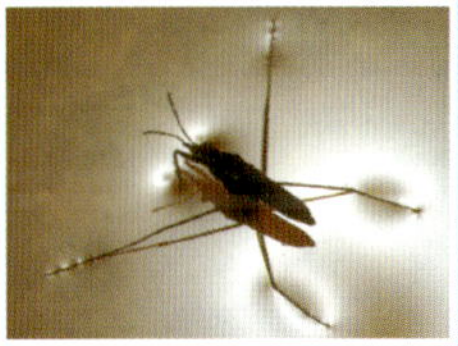

7

Future Vocabulary

- Look at the photograph of the trout ponds on page 6. Say *Each section of the trout ponds seems to be a different color.*

Now revisit pages 8–9

During Reading

Book Talk

- **Comprehension Strategy** Remind children of the Fish Hatchery sign on page 4. Say *Now we learn more about what a hatchery is. It is where the fish hatch out of their eggs.*
- **Phonics Skill** Write *alevins* on the board. Say the word slowly, emphasizing the stressed /a/ in the first syllable and the schwa sound in the second and last syllables. Have children practice saying this word with you and then individually. Repeat for the word *yolk.*
- Point out that some words are in boldfaced type, including two reading vocabulary words, *alevins* and *incubators*. Ask *Where can we look to find out what these words mean?* (the surrounding text, the glossary on page 24, a dictionary)

Turn to page 10 – Book Talk

Chapter 4

In the Hatchery

Dad and I saw the **hatchery** at the trout farm.

We saw lots of tiny trout eggs in special **incubators.**
We could see the eyes of the baby trout inside some of the eggs!

8

an alevin

When baby trout hatch out of their eggs, they are called **alevins.**
At first alevins do not need to eat.
They get all their food from their **yolk sacs.**

Fishy Fact

Trout eggs are called eyed eggs when the eyes of baby trout can be seen inside them.

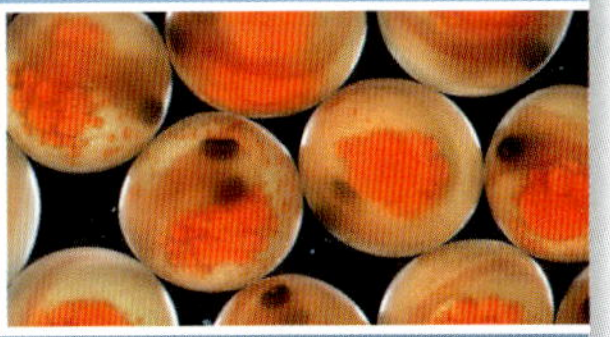

9

Future Vocabulary

- Explain that all living things change as they go through their lifetime. These changes from the beginning of life to the end are called the *life cycle.* Ask *What is the beginning of the life cycle of a trout?* (an egg) *What are trout called in the next stage of their life cycle, after they hatch?* (alevins) Explain that a cycle repeats itself over and over. Every trout has the same life cycle. It is like a circle that goes on and on.
- Say *A bicycle or motorcycle is sometimes called a cycle. Is there any part of a bicycle or motorcycle that is like a life cycle?* (The wheels are like cycles because they are circles that go on and on.)

Now revisit pages 10–11

During Reading

Book Talk

- Ask *How are fry different from alevins?* (Fry are bigger; the egg sac is gone; they eat fish food.)
- **Comprehension Strategy** Say *Look at the photograph on page 11. I wonder what the person is doing. What do you think?* (putting the special trout food in the tanks)
- Ask *Does anyone else have a question? What are you wondering about?* (How big are the fry? Does the person ever fall into the tank?)

Turn to page 12 – Book Talk

Chapter 5

Small Fry

Baby trout grow very quickly.
We saw some baby trout
that were bigger than alevins.
Their yolk sacs were gone.
They had become **fry**.

The fry were swimming around in long tanks. The fry are fed special trout food every day.

Fishy Fact

Trout at trout farms are given special food to help them grow well.

11

Future Vocabulary

- Ask *What are trout called in the next stage of their life cycle?* (fry)
- Point out that the fry stay in long tanks that are divided into sections.

Now revisit pages 12–13

Book Talk

- **Comprehension Strategy** Read the main text on page 13, but do not read the Fishy Fact yet. Say *I wonder how they take the fingerlings to the other farms and lakes.* Read the Fishy Fact, look at the photograph, and say *I think they must carry the fingerlings in a tank like the one in this photograph.*
- Ask *Does anyone else have a question? What are you wondering about?* (Is a fingerling the size of a finger? Why do they let some of the trout go into lakes and rivers?)
- Have children point to any additional glossary words on these pages. Look up *fingerlings*. Have children practice saying the word with you and individually.

Turn to page 14 – Book Talk

Chapter 6

Growing Bigger

Next we looked inside some different tanks. We saw hundreds of little trout!

The trout were bigger than the fry. They had become **fingerlings**.

We learned that most of the fingerlings would stay at the trout farm.

However, some of the fingerlings would go to other trout farms or to lakes or dams.

Fishy Fact

Trout from some trout farms are let go into lakes and rivers.

13

Future Vocabulary

- Ask *What are trout called in the next part of their life* *cycle*, *after they are fry?* (fingerlings)

Now revisit pages 16–17

During Reading

Book Talk

- Ask *Why are the fish in the photograph jumping out of the water?* (to get the food)
- **Comprehension Strategy** Read the text on page 14. Say *When I read page 11, I wondered what the person in the photograph was doing. I thought maybe she was throwing trout food into the tanks. Now I have read on and found out that my answer was probably correct.*

Turn to page 16 – Book Talk

Then we went to a tank full of trout.
We threw some trout food into the water.
Lots of trout jumped up to get the food.

14

The trout were one year old.
They were much bigger than the fingerlings.

We looked at some other tanks.
We saw bigger trout and smaller trout.

Fishy Fact

Bigger and smaller trout are kept in different tanks at trout farms.

During Reading

Book Talk

- Ask *What is the man in the photograph doing?* (putting fish out to sell) *What is the woman doing?* (looking at fish to buy)
- Ask *Why is there ice around the trout in the photographs?* (to keep the trout cold)
- **Comprehension Strategy** Ask *Does anyone have a question about these pages?* (How do they catch the trout? Why is there a green leaf in the fish's mouth? Why are there lemons on the fish?)

Turn to page 18 – Book Talk

Chapter 7

Ready to Eat

When the trout have grown big,
it is time to catch them.
We learned that most of the trout
are sold to markets and restaurants.

Some of the trout are kept at the trout farm. They are sold at the farm store.

We went into the farm store and looked around.

Fishy Fact

Trout must be kept very cold to keep them fresh.

17

Future Vocabulary

- Explain that all of the care and feeding of the trout at the trout farm is to prepare them to be sent to markets and restaurants.
- Point out how the man has arranged the fish in sections in the market display. Ask *Why do you think he has put the fish in different sections?* (different kinds of fish, sizes, prices)
- Ask children to name other foods that are arranged in sections at a market.

Now revisit pages 18–19

During Reading

Book Talk

- **Comprehension Strategy**
Ask *What did the girl and her father use to catch the trout?* (fishing rod, line, hook, bait) *Earlier someone wondered how they catch the trout. Here is how they catch the trout in the special ponds for visitors. We found an answer to the question by reading on.*
- Ask *What word on these pages do you think is in the glossary?* (*bait*) *How do you know?* (It is in boldfaced type.) Together look up and read the definition on page 24.
- Ask *Does anyone else have a question? What are you wondering about?* (Did they have to pay to fish in the special pond? Did they catch any fish?)

Turn to page 20 – Book Talk

Chapter 8

Fishing for Trout

At the farm store, we got some fishing rods and some **bait**.

We went fishing in a special pond at the trout farm.

Dad put some bait on my hook.
Then we put our fishing lines into the pond.

We waited to catch our trout.

Fishy Fact

Many trout farms have special ponds where visitors can go fishing.

19

Future Vocabulary

- Ask *How did the girl and her father prepare to go fishing?* (They bought fishing rods and bait.) *How did the girl's dad prepare her hook for catching trout?* (put bait on her hook)
- Ask children to tell about a time when they prepared for a special activity or outing.

Now revisit pages 20–21

During Reading

Book Talk

- Look at page 20 and ask *Which of these three looks like the trout ponds at the farm the girl visited?* (The raceways look like the ponds pictured on page 5.) *Which look like they might be in a big lake or the sea?* (the big round tanks and the special cages)
- **Comprehension Strategy** Say *I wonder why her dad did not catch any fish. Does anyone else have a question? What are you wondering about?* (Why do trout grow larger in lakes and seas?)

Turn to page 22 – Book Talk

While we were fishing,
Dad told me about other trout farms.
At some trout farms trout are kept in:

long raceways

20

At last I caught
some trout.

Dad did not catch
any trout.
I said he could have
some of mine!

Fishy Fact

The largest trout live in lakes and seas.
They grow much bigger than trout at trout farms.

21

Future Vocabulary

- Talk about the different shapes of the sections shown in the photographs of trout farms. Ask children to name the shapes. (rectangles, circles, squares)

Now revisit pages 22–23

During Reading

Book Talk

- Leave this page spread for children to discover on their own when they read the book individually.

Turn to page 24 – Book Talk

Chapter 9

Our Trout Chart

We had lots of fun at the trout farm. I made a chart, so I will remember what I saw there.

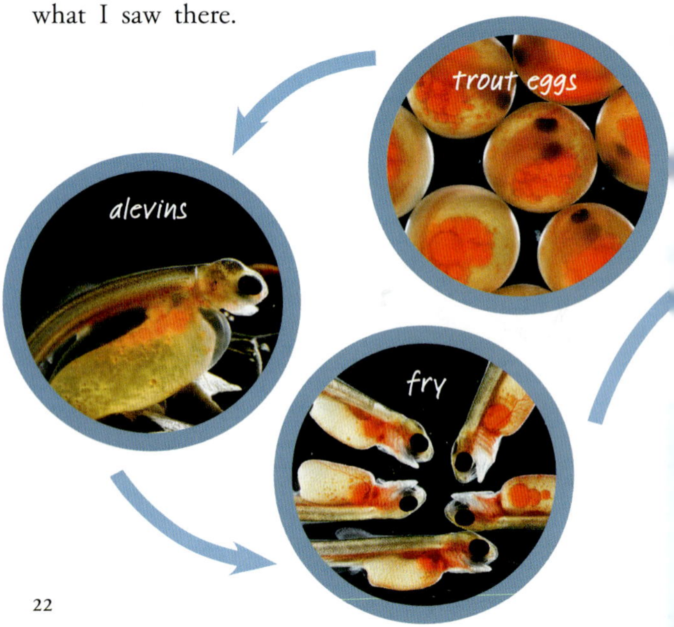

22

Fishy Fact

Trout come from the same family of fish as salmon.

Future Vocabulary

- Ask children what this chart represents. (the life cycle of a trout) Ask *What shape are the sections of the chart?* (circles)
- Ask children to tell about charts or special bulletin board displays they have prepared.

Go to page T5 – Revisiting the Text

Book Talk

* Note: Point out this text feature page as a reference point for children's usage while reading independently.

Individual Reading

Have each child read the entire book at his or her own pace while remaining in the group.

Go to page T5 – Revisiting the Text

Glossary

alevins	baby trout that have just hatched
bait	fish food, used to catch fish
fingerlings	young trout that are older and bigger than alevins or fry
fry	baby trout that are older and bigger than alevins
hatchery	a place where baby trout are hatched from eggs
incubators	special tanks where trout eggs grow and hatch
North America	the third largest continent. The United States is a country in North America.
raceways	long concrete tanks used at fish farms
rainbow trout	a kind of trout with a shiny pink stripe on its sides
yolk sacs	small yellow lumps on new-born alevins that hold food for them

Index

alevins 9–10
eggs 7–9
fingerlings 12–13
fishing 3, 18–20
fry 10–12
hatchery 8
incubators 8
ponds 4–5, 18–19
tanks 11–12, 14–15, 20

24

During independent work time, children can read the online book at:
www.rigbyflyingcolors.com

3 Revisiting the Text

Future Vocabulary

- Use the notes on the right-hand pages to develop oral vocabulary that goes beyond the text. These vocabulary words first appear in future texts. These words are: *prepare*, *sections*, and *cycle*.

Turn back to page 1

Reading Vocabulary Review

Activity Sheet: Word Web

- Have children write *fingerlings* in the center of the Word Web. Model thinking of other things that are small like a finger, such as french fries and worms.
- Have children complete the Word Web with other things that are the size of a finger.

Comprehension Strategy Review

Use Interactive Modeling Card: Main Idea and Supporting Details

- Think aloud about the main idea of the book and ask children to suggest what the main idea is. Write the main idea on the tabletop.
- Model revisiting the book to find a supporting detail and write it on one of the table legs. Together find other supporting details.

Phonics Review

- Have children practice saying *alevins* and *yolk.*
- Talk about ways to decode new words: looking for parts of the word you already know, sounding out, connecting words with pictures.

Fluency Review

- Read the main text on page 9. Point out how you read in phrases rather than word by word and how you paused at the comma. Explain that familiarity with vocabulary words helps you read without stumbling.
- Partner children and have them take turns reading page 9. Encourage children to repeat their reading until they can read smoothly.

Reading-Writing Connection

Activity Sheet: Nonfiction Questions and Answers

To assist children with linking reading and writing:

- Ask children to complete the Activity Sheet, recording what they learned during reading and new questions they have about trout farms.
- With children, use the completed chart to make a list of your own Fishy Facts.

Assessment

Assessing Future Vocabulary

Work with each child individually. Ask questions that elicit each child's understanding of the Future Vocabulary words. Note each child's responses:

- Who prepares breakfast in your home? What does he or she prepare for breakfast?
- Do you ever eat an apple cut into sections? What else do you eat that is in sections?
- A plant has a life cycle, too. What is something that happens during a plant's life cycle?

Assessing Comprehension Strategy

Work with each child individually. Note each child's understanding of asking questions to understand the author:

- What is one question you had while reading *A Day at the Trout Farm*?
- Did you find the answer to your question when you read on in the book? If not, where could you find the answer?
- Why is it good to ask questions while you are reading a book?

Assessing Phonics

Work with each child individually. Give each child word cards for *alevins* and *yolk* and have him or her read each word aloud. Read aloud sentences from pages 9 and 10. Ask the child to point to a word card when he or she hears that word. Note each child's responses for understanding of reading more complex and irregularly spelled words:

- Did each child recognize the words on the word cards and say them accurately?
- Did each child recognize the words when he or she heard them read in a sentence?

Assessing Fluency

Have each child read pages 8 and 9 to you. Note each child's understanding of reading smoothly:

- Was each child able to decode and accurately read the reading vocabulary words and the word *yolk*?
- Did each child say one word at a time or read words in clusters?
- Were each child's junctures between phrases arbitrary or in keeping with sentence meaning and structure?

Interactive Modeling Cards

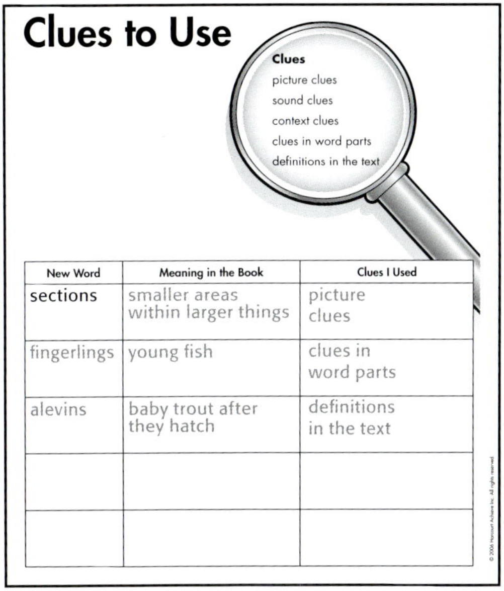

Clues to Use

Clues
picture clues
sound clues
context clues
clues in word parts
definitions in the text

New Word	Meaning in the Book	Clues I Used
sections	smaller areas within larger things	picture clues
fingerlings	young fish	clues in word parts
alevins	baby trout after they hatch	definitions in the text

Directions: With children, fill in the Clues to Use chart using the word *sections* and other words from the text.

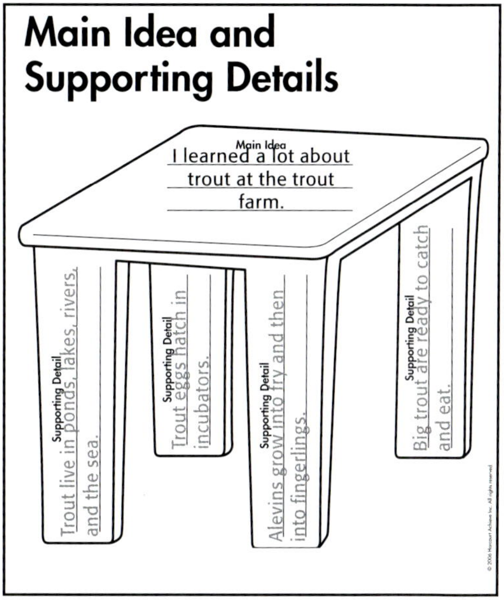

Directions: With children, fill in the Main Idea and Supporting Details chart for *A Day at the Trout Farm.*

Discussion Questions

- On what continent did rainbow trout first live? (Literal)
- Which is bigger, an alevin or a fingerling? How do you know? (Critical Thinking)
- Why do people grow trout on trout farms? Why don't they just catch them in rivers, lakes, and seas? (Inferential)

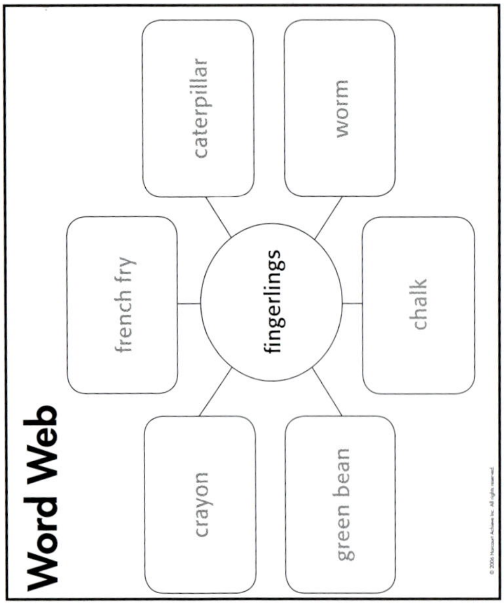

Directions: Have children fill in the Word Web using the word *fingerlings* in the center circle. Have them write names of other things that are the size of a finger in the six boxes.

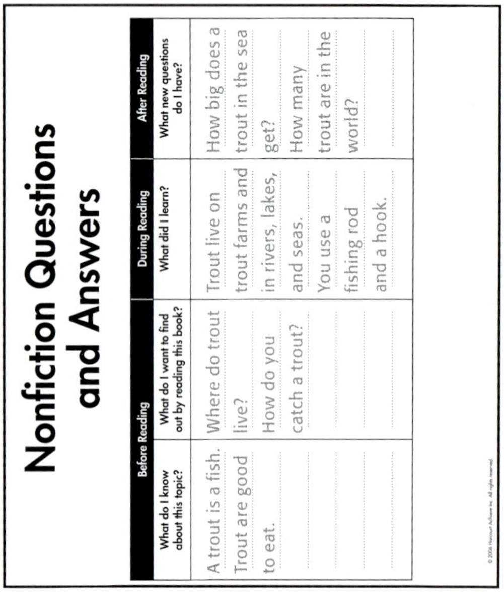
Nonfiction Questions and Answers

Before Reading		During Reading	After Reading
What do I know about this topic?	What do I want to find out by reading this book?	What did I learn?	What new questions do I have?
A trout is a fish. Trout are good to eat.	Where do trout live? How do you catch a trout?	Trout live on trout farms and in rivers, lakes, and seas. You use a fishing rod and a hook.	How big does a trout in the sea get? How many trout are in the world?

Directions: Have children fill in the Nonfiction Questions and Answers chart for *A Day at the Trout Farm.*
Optional: With children, use the completed chart to make a list of your own Fishy Facts.